WITHDRAWN

CYNDI LAUPER

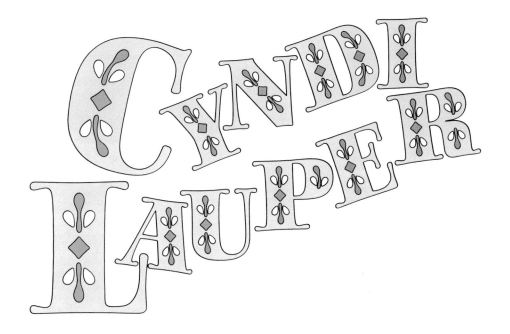

CYNDI LAUPER

by Keith Elliot Greenberg

Lerner Publications Company
Minneapolis

Acknowledgments

Material used in this book was gathered in a first-hand personal interview conducted by the author with Cyndi Lauper as well as from published interviews and articles written by Kurt Loder, Frank Lovece, Margy Rochlin, Dave Zimmer, Todd Gold, John Stark, David Hinckley, and Cathleen McGuigan.

Photos by John Bellissimo/Retna, pp. 2, 6, 20, 24, 26, and 30;
James Shive/Retna, p. 10; Robin Kaplan/Retna, p. 14; Gary Gershoff/Retna, p. 18;
Larry Busacca/Retna, p. 22; Chris Walter/Photo Features International,
front and back covers.

Manufactured in the United States of America

LIBRARY OF CONGRESS CATALOGING IN PUBLICATION DATA

Greenberg, Keith Elliot.
  Cyndi Lauper.

  Summary: Discusses the life and career of the rebellious Grammy Award-winning singer, from her childhood in New York City to her success as a musical performer and rock video star.
    1. Lauper, Cyndi, 1953-   —Juvenile literature.
  2. Rock musicians—United States—Biography—Juvenile literature. [1. Lauper, Cyndi, 1953-
  2. Musicians. 3. Rock music] I. Title.
  ML3930.L18G7   1985   784.5′4′00924 [B] [92]   85-10262
  ISBN 0-8225-1605-5 (lib. bdg.)

1 2 3 4 5 6 7 8 9 10 94 93 92 91 90 89 88 87 86 85

CONTENTS

She's So Unusual   7

A Blue Angel from Queens   11

Going Solo   21

Part of the Human Community   29

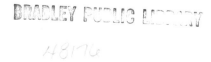

SHE'S
SO UNUSUAL

Cyndi Lauper is a difficult person to figure out. The Grammy Award-winning singer is a rebel who would like to change society, yet her old-fashioned mother is her hero. She's zany, though totally serious about such issues as hungry children in Africa, the disease multiple sclerosis, and women's rights. She's small, but not afraid to step into a wrestling ring and challenge men whom most people call giants.

She's an American success story. Or is she? Although Cyndi seemed to explode onto the international music scene out of nowhere, she has actually been trying to make it as an entertainer for more than ten years. She performed with a number of bands but couldn't capture fame. It wasn't until she was thirty years old that people finally sat up and gave her the attention she had long been seeking.

She's a fashion trendsetter although she never meant to be. Girls all over the world are copying Cyndi's way of presenting herself: trimming their hair close on one side; dying their locks in glow-in-the-dark colors; applying large globs of scarlet make-up over their eyelids and dividing the bright color with a line or two of gold; covering their arms with different-sized and different-shaped bracelets; buying wild earrings; wearing sailor caps, straw hats, strange bonnets and other odd head-wear; putting on clothes that nobody has seen since the 1950s; going to parties in sneakers.

Cyndi has dressed like this for years. Not affected by whichever fad was in, she was just being herself. In fact, before it was elegant to look like Cyndi Lauper, people told her she looked like a bum.

"People used to *throw rocks* at me for my clothes," she remembered. "Now they wanna know where I *buy* 'em, right? Doesn't that seem *weird* to you?"

She sings from the gut. It may sound like she simply steps up to the mike and belts out how she feels, but if you tried singing like Cyndi Lauper, you would discover that it is not easy. She has worked hard to develop her four-octave voice. Music is a passion in her life, and she has studied a variety of styles besides rock'n'roll. Her vocal chords were trained under the careful guidance of an instructor.

"What I sing may seem simple," she said. "But, believe me, it's tricky and hard to hit those high notes every night." Explaining why she rarely makes mistakes in concert, she continued, "I've learned some discipline.

8

I know I have to work on throat and body because I'm a *pipsqueak*. So, you know, I gotta work *hard*."

She's modern. Rock fans, record company executives, and even Cyndi's critics believe her to be a true example of "the 80s woman." But Cyndi's influences come from the past. Many of the singers she admires performed in the 1940s and 1950s and were big favorites of her mother. And the television show she likes best is not "Saturday Night Live," "The Cosby Show" or another current program. It is "The Honeymooners," which was made when she was a baby and can be seen in rerun form on many channels.

If you try to put Cyndi Lauper into a category, you will fail. As newspapers and magazines from Tampa to Tokyo have observed, the only sure thing about her is that she lives up to the title of her first album, *She's So Unusual!*

A BLUE ANGEL FROM QUEENS

America's wackiest redhead since Lucille Ball does not like to discuss her age. "I'm not a car," she commonly snaps when asked how old she is. Promotional material from her old band, Blue Angel, however, lists her date of birth as June 20, 1953. She was born in Boulevard Hospital in Queens, New York, and spent her early years in the shadow of the city's historic Williamsburg Bridge in Brooklyn.

She claims that she started singing around the time she started talking. At a very young age, she would croon along with her mother's *South Pacific* record, lowering her voice to sing the male parts and singing the female parts in a high voice. Sometimes, she'd sing for the old women around the corner from her home. The women enjoyed her performances so much that they tried to reward her with quarters. But her mother did not want

Cyndi taking money from other people, and she forced the girl to return the coins.

Cyndi's father expressed interest in many activities which could be labeled as oddball. A musically inclined man, he showed his talents best with the xylophone. Another hobby to which Cyndi's father devoted time was archaeology. He was not able to put his knowledge about bones and ancient kingdoms to use at his full-time job as a shipping clerk. It is quite possible, though, that his daughter developed a curiosity for offbeat subjects through watching him.

When Cyndi was five, her parents divorced. Cyndi, her older sister, Elen, and younger brother, Butch, all moved with their mother, Catrine Domenique, to the Ozone Park section of Queens. Although Queens is directly across the bridge from the museums, art galleries, and other cultural attractions of Manhattan, Cyndi says that people in her neighborhood rarely took advantage of the numerous opportunities on the other side of the river. She has even described Queens and Manhattan as being like two separate countries.

Life in Ozone Park left much to be desired. Cyndi's family was poor, and her mother was forced to work exhausting twelve-hour shifts as a waitress. Cyndi loved her mother dearly and felt a huge loss every time the woman left the house. After she became successful, Cyndi led a crew from *Life* magazine on a tour of Ozone Park. Suddenly, the singer broke down in tears. "I was so lonely because my mother was working," she cried.

When Catrine was home, she and Cyndi had long chats.

"My mother never shut me up when I wanted to express myself," Cyndi recalled. "That was my saving grace."

Catrine's love for music rubbed off on her children. Cyndi has said that although the family was poor, they "always had music." The voices of old-time artists like Mario Lanza, Billie Holiday, Eileen Farrell, and Louis Armstrong filled the house. Cyndi also enjoyed the sounds of Brenda Lee, Millie Small, and the all-girl groups of the early 60s, such as the Chiffons and the Ronettes. But the group that Cyndi put above all others was the Beatles.

Cyndi and her sister Elen would mimic the Fab Four when they washed dishes. They harmonized "Love Me Do" or "I Want to Hold Your Hand" while one washed and the other wiped. Of course, with their New York accents, they didn't sound much like John Lennon and Paul McCartney, and that disappointed Cyndi.

She was also disappointed with the way she saw women around her leading their lives. She watched girls in the neighborhood go from being pretty, carefree teenagers to angry housewives with too many worries. During holidays, she never liked the way females in her family were kept in the kitchen to cook for the men. Some of the lines in Cyndi's song "Girls Just Want to Have Fun" were influenced by the injustices she noticed at these gatherings.

Cyndi's mother realized that she was selling herself short, like so many other women. Catrine told her daughter, "Don't be afraid of anything you want to be in life. Don't be like me."

Cyndi and her mother just want to have fun.

Cyndi considered her mother good, but the life she led bad. She said, "I figured that if I was bad, I could do, indeed, what I wanted. And if something was good enough for a man to do, then it was good enough for me to do. I decided that I would take any grief anyone would give me as long as I did what I wanted."

At 12, she began rebelling, dying her hair and dressing differently than the other kids. She learned to play Elen's old guitar and started singing. Neighbors complained about her music and insulted her choice of clothes. People began calling her a misfit.

Cyndi admits that she lived up to the label. "No matter how hard I tried to look normal, there was always something that wasn't right," she said. "I'd put on false eyelashes and one would always curl up." The boys she liked, more times than not, liked someone else.

Cyndi was expelled from a local Catholic school and sent to a boarding school at a convent in upstate New York. There she complained about the nuns' strict policies and quickly put herself at odds with the teachers. After six months, she was back in Ozone Park at public school.

Because she had displayed creative talent, Cyndi went to a high school for young artists. Today she claims that her art school background has come in handy when making videos. She compares the video screen to a blank canvas that needs to be filled with people, costumes, and designs. Back then, however, her teachers saw little hope for Cyndi, and she failed many courses.

Like other young rebels in the 60s, Cyndi participated in peace marches and protests against the Vietnam War. But she even found fault with the lack of focus the hippies put on women's rights. "That was the time when people were supposed to be breaking free," Cyndi said. "The only people who were not breaking free were women. I thought it was so unjust."

Cyndi decided to break free from Ozone Park, from school, and from all the things which made her unhappy. At 17, she dropped out of high school and moved out of Queens. Catrine likes to joke that her taste for garlic helped make up Cyndi's mind to leave home. At the time, though, Cyndi was in earnest about her desire to "find herself," and her mother was, naturally, concerned.

Cyndi spent time taking walks and thinking. An artist taught her about painting, politics, and books. To experience the rugged lifestyle Thoreau described in his biography, she went to Canada with her dog, Sparkle, and spent two weeks living in a tent in the woods north of Toronto. Then she moved to Vermont and took art classes at a school near Stowe. She studied for her high school equivalency diploma and supported herself by working as a waitress, a painting class model, a race-track attendant, and even a judo and karate instructor. Her employer didn't mind that her knowledge of the martial arts was extremely limited. About this period of her life, she reflected, "I saw a different kind of culture. I learned."

Cyndi also realized that not only had she run away from Queens, she had run from what she really was: a singer. Determined to start a music career, she returned to Ozone Park. In 1974, she found a job as a backup singer and dancer in a disco band called Doc West. The group did "covers," versions of popular artists' music, at night clubs in Long Island, New York. Cyndi found herself singing the tunes of Chaka Kahn and Labelle as well as performing what she calls a "tacky" tribute to the late Janis Joplin. Her next band, Flyer, specialized in covers of Rod Stewart, the Rolling Stones, and other groups.

But Cyndi didn't really sound like the artists she copied. Her unique style could not be hidden; she moved around the stage more than she was supposed to and sang in her natural voice. Patrons occasionally complained. After a while, Cyndi took the hint. She quit the copy band scene and resolved to record originals of her own.

In 1977, she began taking lessons from Katie Agresta, a classically trained voice coach. Agresta taught her student vocal exercises, put her on a proper diet, and stressed the harmful effects of drugs and alcohol to the throat. Cyndi was a cooperative pupil.

Under Agresta's training, Cyndi's confidence increased. She met John Turi, a keyboardist/saxaphone player/songwriter, and together they started a group called Blue Angel. Within several months, the band's 50s-style music and Cyndi's masterful vocals had convinced executives at Polygram records to offer Blue Angel a contract.

While with Blue Angel, Cyndi became introduced to a man who would later play a major role in her life. She first saw Captain Lou Albano, a heavy-set professional wrestling manager, on an airplane going from San Juan, Puerto Rico, to New York City.

Cyndi, a long-time wrestling fan, was impressed with Albano's "rock'n'roll look"—he wore rubber bands in his black and gray beard. Albano sensed that Cyndi would one day be famous, and he taught her his "P.E.G. principle," which stands for "politeness, etiquette and grooming."

The P.E.G. principle did not help Blue Angel reach the top of the charts. Although critics generally praised the group, its album sold poorly. The band broke up, and Cyndi filed for bankruptcy.

Cyndi sang with Blue Angel for about five years. In 1980, Blue Angel's only album was released. When the band eventually broke up, Cyndi took her time going solo.

Cyndi went back to working at any job that would pay her rent. Dressed as a geisha girl, she sang oldies at a Japanese restaurant. She added touches to her wardrobe while selling clothes at Screaming Mimi's, a second-hand clothing store.

And she continued to dream. In one dream, she was sitting in the backyard of her childhood home, singing to rows of tulips. The flowers were looking up at her and dancing like fans at a rock concert. She knew that good times were ahead.

GOING SOLO

Before beginning her solo career, Cyndi sometimes remembered how hard her mother worked to support the family. Catrine's goal had been to provide for her children, and she accomplished this task successfully. Inspired by her mother's example, Cyndi vowed to put the same amount of energy into her singing.

One important source of help was an understanding man named David Wolff. Wolff had a musical background and was trying to start a career in personal management. From the day he met Cyndi, he found her appealing, both musically and personally. He became her manager and her boyfriend.

Cyndi claims that, since her late teens, she had been hearing a voice that said "Wait till you meet David." Many of the Davids she had met, however, had been

When David Wolff met Cyndi, he was already managing one band, which had been signed by Portrait Records. He introduced Cyndi to the people at Portrait, and the result was *She's So Unusual*.

creeps. When she met Wolff at a party, she first thought him to be a "wise guy." After they talked and had gotten to know each other, however, she realized that *this* was the David she had been waiting for.

With David's help, Cyndi signed a contract with CBS's Portrait records. She put together a band with guitarist/bassist/saxaphone player Eric Bazilian, keyboardist Rob Hyman, drummer Anton Fig, and bassist Neil Jason. Songwriter Jules Shear helped out on the singer's first solo album, *She's So Unusual*, as did producer Robert Chertoff.

The album featured covers of The Brains' "Money Changes Everything" and Prince's "When You Were Mine." Cyndi co-wrote songs like "She-Bop" and rewrote Robert Hazard's "Girls Just Want To Have Fun" from a female point of view.

Above all things, the album had a sense of humor. "Humor is a great vehicle for getting a message across," Cyndi said. She told *Newsweek* magazine, "If you get too serious, you could die of starch."

Cyndi revealed her sense of humor to the American public when she clowned with stars like Johnny Carson and Rodney Dangerfield on national television. Comedian Robert Klein said that she could have been a success in his field. "Her timing is superb," he stated.

"Girls Just Want To Have Fun" is one of the funniest videos ever made. In it, Cyndi's mother, played by Catrine, and father, played by Captain Lou Albano, wring their hands and pace worriedly because of their daughter's free-spirited ways. Cyndi cannot be stopped, though, and she brings an assortment of characters to her room for a party. Among the guests are a conehead, some firemen, Cyndi's real-life brother, Butch, and her dog, Sparkle.

Cyndi hams it up with members of her band.

24

Cyndi's girlfriends in the video are pretty, but not glamorous. She said she wanted to "show the way women really look," not the way men *want* them to look. Because of this point of view, Cyndi has a very large female following.

Her "Time After Time" video, about a boy and girl living in a small town, is serious. David Wolff plays Cyndi's boyfriend and Catrine again plays herself. "Art should reflect life," Cyndi said about the production. She claims that when she and Catrine are crying in the segment, the tears are real.

Wolff also appears in the "She-Bop" video. Like "Girls Just Want To Have Fun," the mood is carefree. Cyndi is arrested by Captain Lou Albano, but not even bars can hold her back from expressing herself. She breaks free to perform a dance number with Wolff.

After "She-Bop" was made, Cyndi had a falling-out with Captain Lou. Albano claimed that he had been totally responsible for the singer's success. "If I wasn't in her videos, people wouldn't have watched them," he boasted. "As it is, they turned off their television sets as soon as the portions involving me were over." He added that a woman's place was in the kitchen.

To prove the Captain wrong, Cyndi began managing female wrestler Wendi Richter. She demanded a match between her charge and the women's champion, handled by Albano. The bout took place in Madison Square Garden in New York. Cyndi led Wendi to the title.

"I'm grateful to Cyndi," Wendi said. "Not only has she given me important tips on wrestling and nutrition.

Wendi Richter (left) outwrestled the Fabulous Moolah (on her head) while Captain Lou Albano and Cyndi managed their two charges from ringside.

She's also helped me learn more about fashion and about being a woman."

Others also expressed their appreciation of Cyndi Lauper. Fans bought close to four million copies of *She's So Unusual*. She was voted "Best New Artist" of 1984 by the Grammy committee, which gives yearly awards to the country's top recording artists. Her music earned five Grammy nominations. She set a new record for female performers by having four Top Five singles on one album. Along with fellow Queens native Geraldine Ferraro, the first female to run for vice president, Cyndi was voted one of the Women of the Year by *Ms.* magazine.

In order to communicate her wishes in the largely male recording business, Cyndi read parts of *The Managerial Woman*, a book for female executives. She claims the book has helped her relate to male executives on their level.

Cyndi believes that, if her mother had had the right opportunities, she might have been able to accomplish a great deal more than she did. For this reason, Cyndi tries to share her success with Catrine. The singer is overjoyed that people recognize her mother from the videos. Cyndi happily told *Rolling Stone* magazine that Catrine now wears sunglasses when she walks Sparkle. "As a matter of fact," the performer added, "Sparkle wears sunglasses now too."

PART OF THE HUMAN COMMUNITY

It has already been said that Cyndi is a firm believer in women's rights. But she does not feel that only women deserve justice. The suffering of any member of the human community pains her, and she has often gone to bat for those less fortunate than herself.

After besting Lou Albano at wrestling management, Cyndi convinced The Captain to mend his evil ways and help her raise money for multiple sclerosis, a disease that currently has no cure. The two traveled to several bars in the New York metropolitan area to clown with patrons and ask for donations. At Studio 54, a glittery disco in Manhattan, the pair judged a contest to pick the "ugliest bartender" in the state. Cyndi pointed out that in this case, ugly stood for "understanding, gorgeous, lovable and youthful."

A representative from the national Multiple Sclerosis Society announced that the duo had raised $100,000 towards a cure for the illness in only two months. Cyndi responded by handing over a check for an additional $5,000. "Honey, money *does* change everything," she told the gathered crowd.

Standing between Albano and World Wrestling Federation heavyweight champion Hulk Hogan, Cyndi stated that she always knew The Captain had a good heart. Touched by the compliment, Albano called the performer "105 pounds of poetry in motion."

Hulk Hogan joined Cyndi at the Grammy Awards when she was honored as Best New Artist.

A few months later, Cyndi joined 45 other artists in an effort to end starvation in Africa. The entertainers recorded a song called "We Are The World," written by Michael Jackson and Lionel Richie, and agreed to donate all money from record sales to a fund for hungry Ethiopians.

It is believed that the eventual proceeds from this effort will total $200 million. Cyndi feels that giving to people on the other side of the world is just as important as giving to people in your neighborhood. Bringing up the name of the late Indian leader Mahatma Gandhi, she said, "Gandhi had the right idea. He is an inspiration to me because of the things he said about the Christians and the Jews and the Muslims and the Hindus and the Buddhists.... He said, 'They're all the same.' That's how I believe. It's a universal thing. Nobody's above or below anyone else."

What does the future hold for Cyndi Lauper? Already, she has gone into the studio to begin work on her next album. Only those very close to the singer know what her new music sounds like, but it was reported that Captain Lou Albano accompanied her on these sessions. Whether they will do a duet together remains to be seen.

Cyndi would like to get involved in filmmaking. She wants to oversee all aspects of a movie: writing, acting, creating the music. If she creates a movie, the cast will be the same team that appears in her videos—Albano, Catrine, Wolff, and maybe even Sparkle. She promises fans that any film she makes will show women in a positive light.

Because so many people are now dressing like Cyndi Lauper, she has begun marketing some of her outfits. She said, "I figured I'd better represent myself in a way that looks good. So I made a couple of little outfits that are really nice, better than the ugly things that some other companies have been puttin' out saying they're *my* style. But really, it's the style of the street, the poor people—which I was one of until recently."

Cyndi's involvement with professional wrestling will also continue. She has urged her friend Mr. T to enlist in the "mat wars." Together, they plan to rid the sport of some of its more treacherous villains.

Of course, the energetic Lauper is always looking for new paths to explore and new worlds to conquer. It is likely that she will continue to be successful, and it is definite that she will continue to keep observers on their toes. No one except Cyndi Lauper will ever be able to predict what Cyndi Lauper will do next.